LET'S LEARN GURMUKHI THROUGH ANIMALS

Sarbdeep Kaur (Parmar) Johal

THIS BOOK BELONGS TO _____

Thank you Baani (My daughter) for inspiring me to write children's books in your mother language (Punjabi). Punjabi Gurmukhi alphabet was standardized during the 16th century by Guru Angad Dev ji, the second Sikh guru. The name Gurmukhi means "from the mouth of the Guru".

I am pleased that this book will inspire many to learn about Punjabi language, culture and heritage. I am extremely grateful for supportive family, friends, my mom, my guiding angel: my daddy ji (Sardaar Baldev Singh), Waheguru ji and my loving husband. This book is dedicated to all the children, especially my curious nieces, nephews, Baani as well as countless students around the world.

The publishing journey would not have been possible without tellwell publishing company and their associates. Thank you Scott Lunn for guiding and answering all the questions during initial stages of the book publication process. I would also like to acknowledge Roxanne Van Gemert for being an awesome project manager. Last but not least Stefanie for bringing my imagination into reality through her astonishing illustrations.

Thank you for all the love and support to the future readers of this book.

"Let the knowledge inspire you to create something beautiful for generations to come"
Sarbdeep Kaur (Parmar) Johal

E eeeε

Aaaaa

ੲ (E)

ਈੜੀ ਦੇਖਦੀ ਇੱਲ
Eir'hee dekh'dee Ei'el
"Eir'hee sees a kite"
Eir'hee says Eeeee

3

ੲ
EIR'HEE

ਸ (S)

ਸੱਸਾ ਦੇਖਦਾ ਸੂਰ
Sa'ssa dekh'da Soor
"Sa'ssa sees a pig"
Sa'ssa says Sssss

Sssss

2

4

ਸ
SA'SSA

ਅ (A)

ਐੜਾ ਦੇਖਦਾ ਅਜਗਰ
Air'ha dekh'da Aja'gar
"Air'ha sees a python"
Air'ha says Aaaaa

ਅ
AIR'HA

Ghhhhh

Kkkkk

④
ਘ
GHU'GHA

ਘ (GH)

ਘੱਘਾ ਦੇਖਦਾ ਘੁੱਗੀ
Ghu'gha dekh'da Ghoo'ghi
"Ghu'gha sees a dove"
Ghu'gha says Ghhhhh

①
ਕ
KAKKA

ਕ (K)

ਕੱਕਾ ਦੇਖਦਾ ਕੀੜੀ
Ka'kka dekh'da Kirh'ee
"Ka'kka sees an ant"
Kakka says Kkkkk

③
ਗ
GA'G

ਗ (G)

ਗੱਗਾ ਦੇਖਦਾ ਗੀਂਡੋਆ
Ga'gga dekh'da Gun'doa
"Ga'gga sees an earthworm"
Ga'gga says Ggggg

ਜ (J)

ਜੱਜਾ ਦੇਖਦਾ ਜਾਲੇ ਵਿੱਚ ਮੱਕੜੀ

Ja'jja dekh'da Jaal'ey vich maka'rhi

"Ju'jja sees a spider web"

Ju'jja says Jjjjj

ਜ
JU'JJA

Jjjjj

ਛ (CHH/SHH)

ਛੱਛਾ ਦੇਖਦਾ ਛੋਟਾ ਕੱਛੂ

Chhu'chha dekh'da sho'ta kat'shu

"Chhu'chha sees a small turtle"

Chhu'chha says CHHhhhh

ਛ
CHHU'CHHA

CHHhhhh

CHH

ਞ (NJ)

Nj'anj'a ਖਾਲੀ

Kha'ali

Empty

Njanj'a is not used to begin a word

ਞ
KHA'ALI

ਟ (T)

ਟੈਂਕਾ ਦੇਖਦਾ ਟਿੱਡਾ
Tain'ka dekh'da Tee'da
"Tain'ka sees a grasshopper"
Tain'ka says Ttttt

TAIN'KA

Ttt

Ddddd

KHA 'ALI

ਣ (NH)

Nah'nha ਖਾਲੀ
Kha'lee
Empty
Nah'nha is not used to begin a word

DU'DDA

ਡ (D)

ਡੱਡਾ ਦੇਖਦਾ ਡੱਡੂ
Du'dda dekh'da Da'doo
"Du'dda sees a frog"
Du'dda says Ddddd

ਧ (DH)

ਧੱਧਾ ਦੇਖਦਾ ਧੱਗੀ
Dhu'hdha dekh'da Dhu'gee
"Dhu'hdha sees a female cow"
Dhu'hdha says DHhhhh

DHhhhh

4

ਧ
DHU'HDHA

THhhhh

2

ਠ
THU'HTHA

ਠ (TH)

ਠੱਠਾ ਦੇਖਦਾ ਨੂਹਾਂ
Thu'htha dekh'da Thoo'ha
"Thu'htha sees a scorpion"
Thu'htha says THhhhh

ਤ (T)

ਤੱਤਾ ਦੇਖਦਾ ਤਿੱਤਲੀ

Tuh'ta dekh'da tit'lee

"Tuh'ta sees a butterfly"

Tuh'ta says Ttttt

① ਤ TUH'TA

THhhhh

② ਥ THU'HTHA

ਥ (Th)

ਥੱਥਾ ਦੇਖਦਾ ਥੈਲਾ ਕੰਗਾਰੂ ਦਾ

Thu'htha dekh'da Th'ella kan'garoo da

"Thu'htha sees a Kangaroo pouch"

Thu'htha says THhhhh

Nnnnn

ਨ (N)

ਨੱਨਾ ਦੇਖਦਾ ਨਿਊਲਾ

Nuh'na dekh'da nee'oo'la

"Nuh'na sees a mongoose"

Nuh'na says Nnnnn

⑤ ਨ NUH 'NA

ਧ (DH)

ਧੱਧਾ ਦੇਖਦਾ ਧਮੋੜੀ

<u>Dhu'dda dekh'da Dha'mo'rhee</u>

"Dhu'dda sees a wasp"

Dhu'dda says DHhhhh

ਦ (D)

ਦੱਦਾ ਦੇਖਦਾ ਦਰਿਆਈ ਘੋੜਾ

<u>Du'hda dekh'da dari'aye Gho'rha</u>

"Du'hda sees a hippopotamus"

Du'hda says Ddddd

Mmmmm

BHhhh

ਮ (M)

ਮੌਮਾ ਦੇਖਦਾ ਮੱਛੀ
Mumma dekh'da Ma'chhee
"Mumma sees a fish"
Mumma says Mmmmm

ਮ
MUMMA ⑤

Ppppp

ਪ (P)

ਪੱਪਾ ਦੇਖਦਾ ਪੰਛੀ
Puppa dekh'da Pan'sh'ee
"Pupp'a sees a bird"
Pupp'a says Ppppp

ਪ
PUPP'A ①

PH hhhh

4

ਭ
BHU'HBHA

ਭ (BH)

ਭੱਭਾ ਦੇਖਦਾ ਭੇਡ
Bhu'hbha dekh'da Bhed
"Bhu'hbha sees a sheep"
Bhu'hbha says BHhhhh

2

ਫ
PHU'PHA

ਫ (PH)

ਫੱਫਾ ਦੇਖਦਾ ਫੁੱਲ-ਚੁੰਗੀ
Phu'pha dekh'da Phul-Chu'gee
"Phu'pha sees a sun-bird"
Phu'pha says PHhhhh

Bhbbb

3

ਬ
BU 'BA

ਬ (B)

ਬੱਬਾ ਦੇਖਦਾ ਬਿੱਲੀ
Bu'ba dekh'da Bill'ee
"Bu'ba sees a cat"
Bu'ba says Bbbbb

ਯ (Y)

ਯਆਈਆ ਦੇਖਦਾ ਯਾਕ
Yai'aa dekh'da Yak
"Yai'aa sees a yaak"
Yai'aa says Yyyyy

Yyyyy

1
ਯ
YAI'AA

ੜ (RH)

Rh'arh'a ਖਾਲੀ/
Kha'lee
Empty
Rah'rha is not used to begin a word

5 ੜ
KHA'ALI

LLLLL

ਲ (L)

ਲੱਲਾ ਦੇਖਦਾ ਲੂੰਬੜੀ
Lu'llha dekh'da Loom'barhi
"Lu'llha sees a fox"
Lullha says Lllll

3 ਲ
LULLHA

Rrrrr

Wwwww

2

ਰ
RU'HRRA

ਰ (R)

ਰੱਗਾ ਦੇਖਦਾ ਰਿੱਛ
Ru'hrra dekh'da Rish
"Ru'hrra sees a bear"
Ru'hrra says Rrrrr

4

ਵ
WAWA

ਵ (w/v)

ਵਾਵਾ ਦੇਖਦਾ ਵਾਲਰਸ
Wawa dekh'da walrus
"Wawa sees a walrus"
Wawa says Wwwww

ੜ (LH)

Lh'alh'a ਖਾਲੀ/
Kha'lee
Empty
Lh'alha is not used to begin a word

ਲ਼
KHA'ALI
6

GHaaaa

ਗ (GH'A)

ਗੱਗਾ ਦੇਖਦਾ ਤੇਗ਼ਾਮੱਛੀ
Guh'gh'a dekh'da Tega' mash'ee
"Guh'gh'a sees a swordfish"
Guh'gh'a says GH'aaaa

JH.

KHaaa

PHaaaa

ਗ਼ਾ
GUH'GH'A
3

ਫ (FA'H)

ਫੱਫਾ ਦੇਖਦਾ ਫਨੀਅਰ
Phuh'pha dekh'da Phaa'niar
"Phuh'pha sees a snake cobra"
Phu'pha says PH'aaaa

ਫ਼ੑ
PHU'PHA
5

ਖ਼
KHU'HKHA
2

ਜ਼ (JH'A)

ਜ਼ੱਜ਼ਾ ਦੇਖਦਾ ਜ਼ੈਬਰਾ

<u>Juhjh'a dekh'da Jeyba'ra</u>

"Juh'jh'a sees a Zebra"

Juh'jh'a says JH'aaaa

ਸ਼ (SH'A)

ਸ਼ੱਸ਼ਾ ਦੇਖਦਾ ਸ਼ੇਰ

<u>Shusha dekh'da Sher</u>

"Shush'a sees a lion"

Shush'a says SH'aaaa

ਖ਼ (KH'A)

ਖੱਖਾ ਦੇਖਦਾ ਖ਼ਰਗੋਸ਼

<u>Khu'hkha dekh'da Khur'gosh</u>

"Khu'hkha sees a rabbit"

Khu'hkha says KH'aaaa

"ਗੁਰਮੁੱਖੀ ਲਿੱਪੀ" :"Gurmukhi Lippi"

"Punjabi Alphabets"

ੳ: (O/U) Ur'ha

ਅ: (A) Air'ha

ੲ: (E) Eir'hee

ਸ: (S) Sa'ssa

ਹ: (H) Hahha

ਕ (K) Ka'kka

ਖ (KH) Khu'kha

ਗ (G) Ga'gga

ਘ (GH) Ghu'gha

ਙ (NG) N'ganga

ਚ (CH) Chu'cha

ਛ (CHH/SHH) Chhu'chha

ਜ (J) Ja'jja

ਝ (JH) Jhu'jha

ਞ (NJ) Nj'anj'a

ਟ (T) Tain'ka

ਠ (TH) Thu'htha

ਡ (D) Du'dda

ਢ (DH) Dhu'hdha

ਣ (NH) Nah'nha

ਤ (T) Tuh'ta

ਥ (Th) Thu'htha

ਦ (D) Du'hda

ਧ (DH) Dhu'dda

ਨ (N) Nuh'na

ਪ (P) Puppa

ਫ (PH) Phu'pha

ਬ (B) Bu'ba

ਭ (BH) Bhu'hbha

ਮ (M) Mumma

ਯ (Y) Yai'aa

ਰ (R)Ru'hrra

ਲ (L) Lu'llha

ਵ (w/v) Wawa

ੜ (RH) Rh'arh'a

ਸ਼ (SH'A) Sa'ssey pai'er bindi: Sh'a boll'ey

ਖ਼ (KH'A) Khu'khey pai'er bindi: Kh'a boll'ey

ਗ਼ (GH'A) Ga'ggey pai'er bindi: Gh'a boll 'ey

ਜ਼ (JH'A) Ju'jjey pai'er bindi: Jh'a boll'ey

ਫ਼ (FA'H) Phuh'phey pai'er bindi: Fa'hboll'ey

ਲ਼ (LH) Lu'llhey pai'er bindi: LH boll'ey

By : Sarbdeep Kaur (Parmar) Johal

Tellwell Talent
www.tellwell.ca

ISBN 978-1-77302-882-8 (Paperback)

CPSIA information can be obtained
at www.ICGtesting.com
Printed in the USA
LVHW070254010322
712157LV00012B/82